Pumpkin the Cat - Alley Cat to City Kitty
Children's Book About Pet Loss

Written by Keeley Kincaid
Illustrated by Mehanun Nesa Era
www.keeleykincaid.com
keeley@keeleykincaid.com

© 2025 Keeley Kincaid. All rights reserved.
No part of this publication may be reproduced, stored in a retrieval system, or transmitted in any form or by any means—electronic, mechanical, photocopy, recording, or otherwise—without the prior written permission of the publisher, except for brief quotations used in reviews or scholarly works.

This is a work of creative nonfiction inspired by the real-life adventures of Pumpkin the Cat. Some details have been adapted for storytelling purposes.

For information about bulk purchases, school visits, or author appearances, please contact: keeley@keeleykincaid.com

First Edition
ISBN: 979-8-218-70622-7 (hardcover)
ISBN: 979-8-218-65488-7 (paperback)

PUMPKIN THE CAT

Alley Cat to City Kitty

Children's Book About Pet Loss

Written by Keeley Kincaid

Illustrated by Meharun Nesa Era

A LEGEND IS BORN

In the alleys of Birmingham, where shadows danced and secrets hid, there was a **cat like no other.** With fur as orange as the setting sun and a tail that waved like a flag, Pumpkin ruled the streets.

"A legend has arrived!" whispered the sparrows.

LIFE IN THE ALLEY

Pumpkin enjoyed life in his alley.

He napped in sunny spots, chased the fluttering leaves, and greeted everyone with a **cheerful meow.**

But deep down, he dreamed of
a **cozy home** where he could be loved.

A ROCKY START

Pumpkin's journey to finding a home **wasn't easy.**

The first family who adopted him had a little boy who loved Pumpkin dearly. But soon, they discovered that the boy was **allergic to cats.**

To keep everyone happy, they let Pumpkin roam behind the apartment building, in the alley where he came from.

All the neighbors treated Pumpkin like a friendly stray
and soon a new family began feeding him
and giving him affection,
but never let him inside.

Pumpkin really liked this family and often returned to their door.
But one day, when Pumpkin came back,
this family had moved!

Pumpkin wasn't alone for long. One sunny afternoon, a kind lady saw him on her porch, looking tired but hopeful.

She knelt down and said, **"Hello, little kitty!"**

And Pumpkin tilted his head,
as if to say, **"Are you the one?"**

WELCOME HOME, PUMPKIN

Pumpkin's new home was everything he'd ever dreamed of. There were sunny windows, soft blankets, and delicious treats.

"**This is my kingdom now!**" Pumpkin purred, curling up on the comfiest chair.

PARTY ANIMAL

Pumpkin loved a good party! When guests arrived, he greeted them all, winding through legs and accepting pets.

He'd sit by the food, giving his best
'feed me' eyes until someone shared a bite.

CITY KITTY ADVENTURES

Pumpkin's adventures didn't stop there! He moved to New York City, where he became a true city kitty! He watched the yellow taxis zoom by, greeted neighbors on the stoop, and even got his own seat by the window to watch the **world go by.**

A BELOVED FRIEND TO ALL

Pumpkin had a gift—he made friends wherever he went. Whether it was a neighbor, a stranger, or even another cat, everyone loved him.

"He's like sunshine in fur," people would say, and Pumpkin soaked up the attention.

A BRAVE HEART

As Pumpkin grew older, he faced new challenges. His kidneys needed extra care so his mom and his Irish Nanny, Gwen, worked together to make sure he was comfortable and happy. Gwen gave Pumpkin special fluids and medicine, and he purred through it all, **as brave as ever.**

While Pumpkin's mom was away, Gwen, had an idea. She asked Darrell the doorman for special permission to take Pumpkin to the **rooftop garden**—and he said yes.

It was the perfect reward for **Pumpkin's bravery.** Surrounded by flowers and sunshine, he sniffed the air, listened to the birds, and soaked it all in.
He loved every minute of it.

CHERISHING EVERY MOMENT

As Pumpkin's days grew quieter, he was **surrounded with love** showered with extra snuggles, soft blankets, and all his favorite treats.

After that first visit to the rooftop, it became Pumpkin's favorite thing to do. **Each morning,** he stretched out among the flowers, soaking up the sun and listening to the birds. He watched the city wake up, calm and content.

He may not have been as quick on his paws, but his heart was full. Pumpkin had lived a life of adventure, love, and friendship—
just as it was meant to be.

THE RAINBOW BRIDGE

When it was time to say goodbye, Pumpkin lay surrounded by love. As he crossed the rainbow bridge, the world felt quieter, but his spirit glowed brighter than ever.

"You were my sweetest friend," whispered his mom.

THE LEGEND LIVES ON

Pumpkin's story doesn't end here. In every sunny nap, every kind gesture, and every joyful purr, his spirit lives on. He taught us to love, to laugh, and to live life with paws in the air. Pumpkin wasn't just a cat—
he was a legend.

THE REAL PUMPKIN

Pumpkin wasn't just a cat. He was a companion, a character, and a little orange legend. In the alleys of Birmingham, he was known by many names: Orange Kitty, Opie Jack, and Poncho. But when he chose his forever home, he became Pumpkin.

From that moment on, he lived a big, beautiful life. In New York City, he was loved by neighbors who brought him treats and stopped to say hello. When his mom traveled, his Irish nanny Gwen cared for him with devotion and shared his adventures with friends worldwide. When Pumpkin crossed the Rainbow Bridge, messages of love poured in from near and far.

One of Pumpkin's favorite places was the rooftop garden. Every morning, Darrell the doorman opened it early just for him. With his mom and Gwen by his side, Pumpkin would stretch out among the flowers, soak in the sun, and watch the city wake up.

This book is a tribute to a life filled with joy, friendship, and deep, lasting love. If you've ever loved a pet like Pumpkin, may his story remind you of your own and how that love never truly leaves us.

Pumpkin & Keeley
on the Rooftop New York City,
Upper East Side

Summer of 2020

Thank you so much for picking up this book and sharing it with your little one. It truly means the world to me that you've chosen a story that I hope brought a bit of comfort, connection, or even a quiet moment together. If you have a moment, I'd be so grateful if you left an honest review wherever you purchased the book—your feedback helps more than you know.

And if you're ever in the mood to slow down and get creative, I'd love for you to check out my coloring books at www.keeleykincaid.com—they're made with the same love and care as this book.

With love,
Keeley

www.ingramcontent.com/pod-product-compliance
Lightning Source LLC
Chambersburg PA
CBHW061356010526
44107CB00012B/948